EASY POP MELODIES
FOR RECORDER

ISBN 978-1-4803-8439-2

HAL•LEONARD®
CORPORATION

7777 W. BLUEMOUND RD. P.O. BOX 13819 MILWAUKEE, WI 53213

Visit Hal Leonard Online at
www.halleonard.com

4	All My Loving		34	My Cherie Amour
5	Beauty and the Beast		36	My Favorite Things
6	Blowin' in the Wind		35	My Girl
7	Can You Feel the Love Tonight		38	My Heart Will Go On (Love Theme from 'Titanic')
8	Can't Help Falling in Love		39	Nights in White Satin
9	Clocks		40	Nowhere Man
10	Daydream Believer		41	Puff the Magic Dragon
11	Don't Know Why		42	Raindrops Keep Fallin' on My Head
12	Don't Stop Believin'		43	Scarborough Fair/Canticle
14	Edelweiss		44	Somewhere Out There
15	Eight Days a Week		46	The Sound of Music
16	Every Breath You Take		48	Strangers in the Night
17	Fireflies		49	Sunshine on My Shoulders
18	Georgia on My Mind		50	Sweet Caroline
20	Hey, Soul Sister		51	Till There Was You
22	Hot N Cold		52	The Times They Are A-Changin'
19	In My Life		54	Tomorrow
24	Isn't She Lovely		53	Unchained Melody
25	The Letter		56	Viva la Vida
26	Like a Virgin		58	We Are the World
27	The Look of Love		59	What a Wonderful World
28	Love Me Tender		60	Wonderwall
30	Love Story		62	You Are the Sunshine of My Life
29	Mr. Tambourine Man		63	You've Got a Friend
32	Moon River			
33	Morning Has Broken			

ALL MY LOVING

RECORDER

Words and Music by JOHN LENNON
and PAUL McCARTNEY

BEAUTY AND THE BEAST

from Walt Disney's BEAUTY AND THE BEAST

RECORDER

Lyrics by HOWARD ASHMAN
Music by ALAN MENKEN

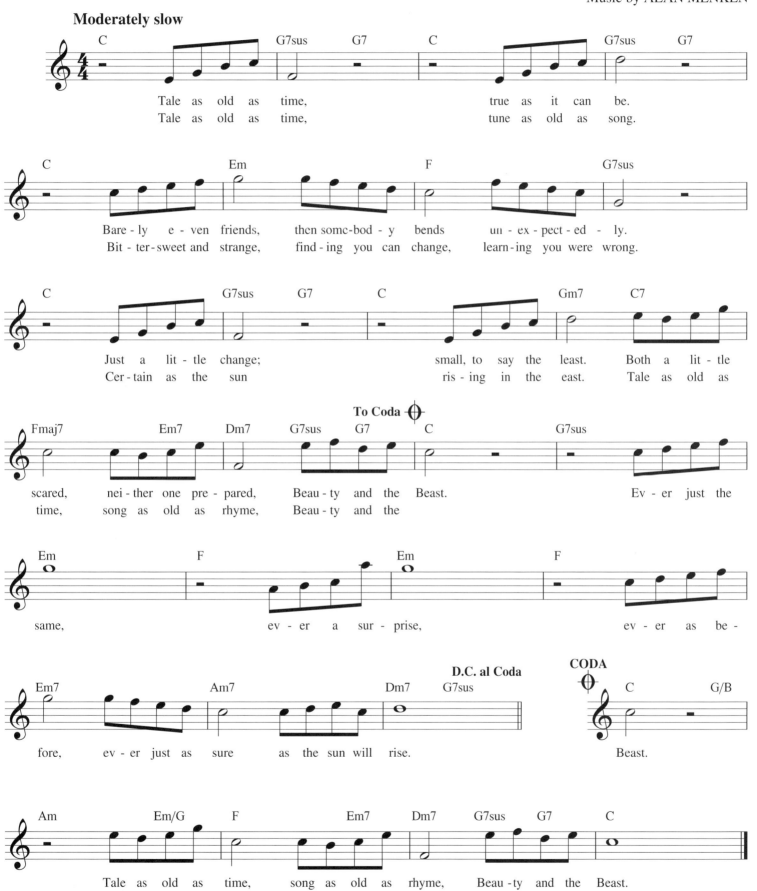

BLOWIN' IN THE WIND

RECORDER

Words and Music by
BOB DYLAN

CAN YOU FEEL THE LOVE TONIGHT

from Walt Disney Pictures' THE LION KING

RECORDER

Music by ELTON JOHN
Lyrics by TIM RICE

CAN'T HELP FALLING IN LOVE

RECORDER

Words and Music by GEORGE DAVID WEISS,
HUGO PERETTI and LUIGI CREATORE

CLOCKS

Words and Music by GUY BERRYMAN,
JON BUCKLAND, WILL CHAMPION
and CHRIS MARTIN

RECORDER

DAYDREAM BELIEVER

RECORDER

Words and Music by
JOHN STEWART

DON'T KNOW WHY

RECORDER

Words and Music by
JESSE HARRIS

Moderately

I wait-ed till ___ I saw the sun.   Don't know why ___ I
When I saw ___ the break of day,   wished that I ___ could
Some-thing has ___ to make you run.   Don't know why ___ I

did-n't come.   Left you by ___ the house of fun.
fly a-way   'stead of kneel-ing in the sand,
did-n't come.   Feel as emp-ty as a drum.

1.

Don't know why ___ I did-n't come.   I don't know why ___ I

Fine   **2.**

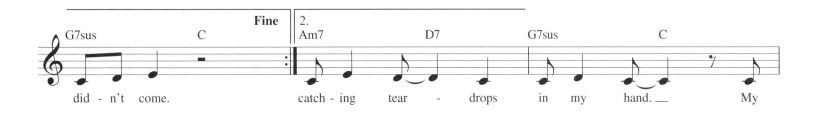

did-n't come.   catch-ing tear-drops in my hand. ___ My

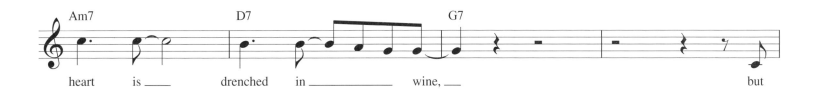

heart is ___ drenched in ___ wine, ___ but

D.S. al Fine
(take 1st ending)

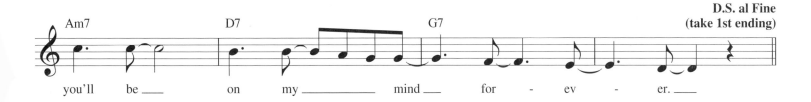

you'll be ___ on my ___ mind ___ for-ev-er. ___

DON'T STOP BELIEVIN'

RECORDER

Words and Music by STEVE PERRY,
NEAL SCHON and JONATHAN CAIN

EDELWEISS

from THE SOUND OF MUSIC

RECORDER

Lyrics by OSCAR HAMMERSTEIN II
Music by RICHARD RODGERS

EIGHT DAYS A WEEK

RECORDER

Words and Music by JOHN LENNON
and PAUL McCARTNEY

Moderately fast

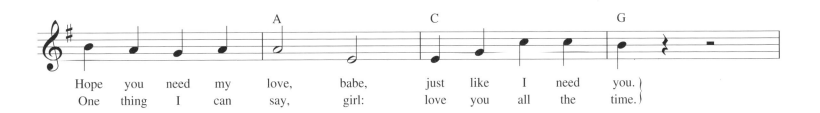

1., 3. Ooh, I need your love, babe; guess you know it's true.
2. Love you ev - 'ry day, girl; al - ways on my mind.

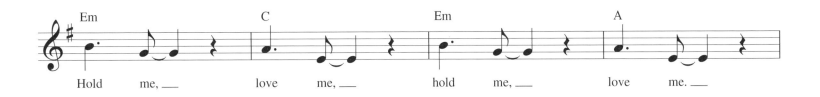

Hope you need my love, babe, just like I need you.
One thing I can say, girl: love you all the time.

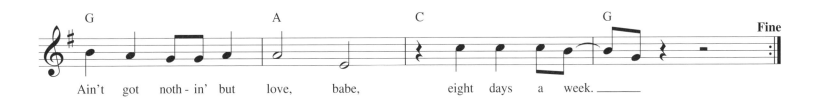

Hold me, ___ love me, ___ hold me, ___ love me. ___

Ain't got noth - in' but love, babe, eight days a week. ___

Eight days a week I love ___ you.

Eight days a week is not e - nough to show I care. ___

EVERY BREATH YOU TAKE

RECORDER

Music and Lyrics by
STING

Moderately

Ev - 'ry breath you __ take, ev - 'ry move you __ make,
Ev - 'ry move you __ make, ev - 'ry vow you __ break,

ev - 'ry bond you break, ev - 'ry step you take, I'll be watch - ing you.
ev - 'ry smile you fake, ev - 'ry claim you stake, I'll be watch - ing you.

Ev - 'ry sin - gle __ day, ev - 'ry word you __ say,

ev - 'ry game you play, ev - 'ry night you stay, I'll be watch-ing you.

Oh, can't you __ see you be - long to __ me?

How my poor heart __ aches __ with ev - 'ry step __ you take.

FIREFLIES

RECORDER

Words and Music by
ADAM YOUNG

GEORGIA ON MY MIND

Recorder

Words by STUART GORRELL
Music by HOAGY CARMICHAEL

IN MY LIFE

RECORDER

Words and Music by JOHN LENNON
and PAUL McCARTNEY

HEY, SOUL SISTER

RECORDER

Words and Music by PAT MONAHAN,
ESPEN LIND and AMUND BJORKLAND

Hey, _____ hey, _____ hey. _____

_____ Your lip - stick stains on the front lobe of my
Just in time, I'm so glad you have a

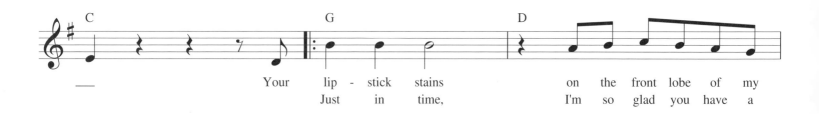

left - side brains. I know I wouldn't for - get ya, and so I went and
one - track mind like me. You gave my life di - rec - tion, a game show love con -

let you blow ___ my mind. ___ Your
nec - tion we can't de - ny. ___ I'm

sweet moon - beam, the smell of you in ev - 'ry sin - gle dream I dream. _
so ob - sessed; my heart is bound to beat right out my un - trimmed chest. _

I knew when we col - lid - ed you're the one I have de - cid - ed who's one of my kind. __
I be - lieve in you; like a vir - gin, you're Ma - don - na, and I'm al - ways gon - na

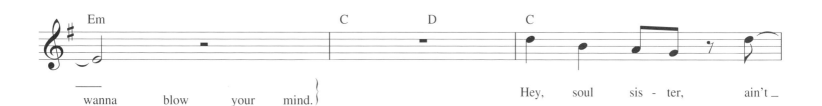

wanna blow your mind. Hey, soul sis - ter, ain't __

that Mis - ter Mis - ter on the ra - di - o, ster - e - o? The way you move ain't fair, you know.

Hey, soul sis - ter, I __ don't wan - na miss a sin - gle thing you do __

to - night. Hey, __ hey, __

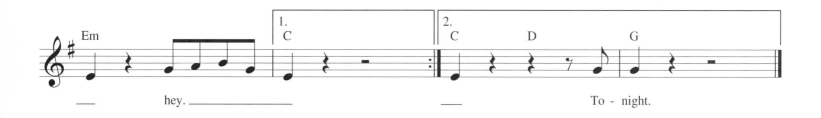

hey. __ To - night.

HOT N COLD

RECORDER

Words and Music by KATY PERRY,
MAX MARTIN and LUKASZ GOTTWALD

You change your mind ___ like a girl ___ chang-es clothes. ___
We used to be ___ just like twins, ___ so in sync. ___

___ Yeah, you P - M - S ___ like a girl, ___
___ The same en - er - gy ___ now's a dead ___

___ I would know. ___ And you o - ver - think, ___
___ bat - ter - y. ___ Used to laugh 'bout noth - ing; ___

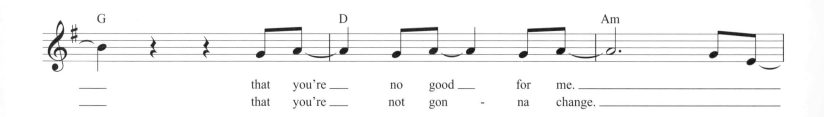

___ al - ways speak ___ cryp - tic - 'ly. ___ I should know ___
now you're plain ___ bor - ing. ___ I should know ___

G   D   Am
___ that you're ___ no good ___ for me.
___ that you're ___ not gon - na change.

'Cause you're hot ___ then you're cold. You're yes ___ then you're no. You're in ___

___ then you're out. You're up ___ then you're down. You're wrong ___ when it's right. It's black ___

___ and it's white. We fight, ___ we break up. We kiss, ___ we make up. ___

You don't real - ly wan - na stay, no, ___ but you don't real - ly wan - na

go. _____ You're hot ___ then you're cold. You're yes ___ then you're no. You're in ___

___ then you're out. You're up ___ then you're down. _

___ then you're down. _

ISN'T SHE LOVELY

RECORDER

Words and Music by
STEVIE WONDER

Bright Shuffle

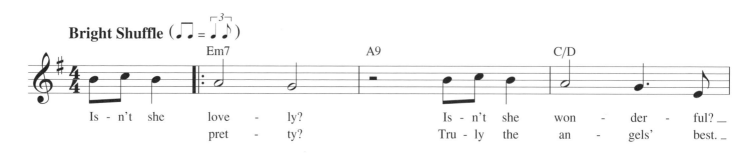

Is - n't she love - ly? / pret - ty?   Is - n't she won - der - ful? / Tru - ly the an - gels' best. _

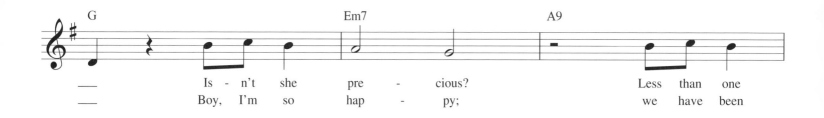

___ Is - n't she pre - cious?   Less than one
___ Boy, I'm so hap - py;   we have been

min - ute old. ___   I nev - er thought ___ through love we'd be ___
heav - en blessed. __   I can't be - lieve ___ what God has done. _

___ mak - ing one as love - ly ___ as she. ___ }   But is - n't she
___ Through us He's giv - en life ___ to one. ___ }

love - ly? Made from love.   **1.** Is - n't she   **2.**

THE LETTER

Recorder

Words and Music by
WAYNE CARSON THOMPSON

Moderately

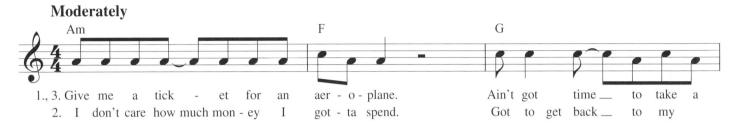

1., 3. Give me a tick - et for an aer - o - plane.
2. I don't care how much mon - ey I got - ta spend.
Ain't got time _ to take a
Got to get back _ to my

fast _ train.
ba - by again.
Lone - ly days are gone; _ I'm a - go - in' home. _ Oh, my

ba - by just wrote me a let - ter.
- ter.

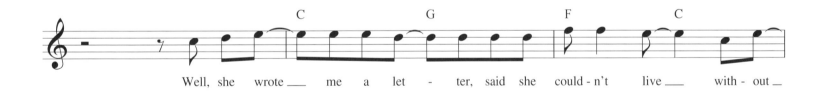

Well, she wrote _ me a let - ter, said she could - n't live _ with - out _

_ me no more.
Lis - ten, mis - ter, can't you see I

D.C. al Fine
(take 1st ending)

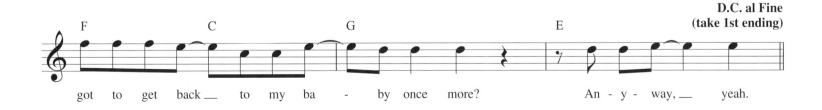

got to get back _ to my ba - by once more?
An - y - way, _ yeah.

LIKE A VIRGIN

RECORDER

Words and Music by BILLY STEINBERG
and TOM KELLY

THE LOOK OF LOVE

from CASINO ROYALE

RECORDER

Words by HAL DAVID
Music by BURT BACHARACH

LOVE ME TENDER

RECORDER

Words and Music by ELVIS PRESLEY
and VERA MATSON

Moderately

Love me ten - der, love me sweet; nev - er let me
Love me ten - der, love me long; take me to your

go. You have made my life com - plete,
heart. For it's made there my that I be - long,

and I love you so. ⎱ Love me ten - der,
and we'll nev - er part. ⎰

love me true. All my dreams ful - fill.

For, my dar - ling, I love you, and I al - ways

will. and I al - ways will.

MR. TAMBOURINE MAN

RECORDER

Words and Music by
BOB DYLAN

Hey, Mis - ter Tam - bou - rine Man, play a song for me. I'm not
sleep - y and there is no place I'm go - ing to.
Hey, Mis - ter Tam - bou - rine Man, play a song for me. In the
jin - gle jan - gle morn - ing I'll come fol - low - ing you.

Though I know this eve - ning's em - pire has re - turned in - to
wea - ri - ness a - maz - es me. I'm brand - ed on my

sand, van - ished from my hand, left me blind - ly here to
feet. I have no one to meet, and the an - cient emp - ty

stand but still not sleep - ing, my
street's too dead for dream - ing.

LOVE STORY

RECORDER

Words and Music by
TAYLOR SWIFT

We were both young when I first saw __ you. I close my eyes __ and the

flash-back starts. _ I'm stand-ing there on a bal-co-ny in sum-mer air.

See the lights, _ see the par - ty, the ball __ gowns. See you make __ your way

I sneak out __ to the gar - den to see __ you. We keep qui - et 'cause we're

through the crowd _ and say hel - lo. Lit - tle did I _____ know

dead if they knew, _ so close your eyes, es - cape this town for a lit - tle while.

that you were Ro - me - o. You were throw - ing peb - bles, and my

'Cause you were Ro - me - o; I was the scar - let let - ter. And my

dad - dy said, "Stay a - way from Ju - li - et." __ And I was cry - ing on the stair - case,

dad - dy said, "Stay a - way from Ju - li - et." __ But you were ev - 'ry - thing to me. I was

beg - ging you, please, _ don't go. _____ And I _____ said:

Ro - me - o, take me some-where we can be a - lone. I'll be wait - ing.

All there's left to do is run. You'll be the prince and I'll be the prin - cess.

It's a love sto - ry. ___ Ba - by, just say yes. So

Ba - by, just say ___ yes. _____ Oh, ___ oh, oh. ___

Oh, ___ oh, oh, _____ oh.

'Cause we were both young when I first saw ___ you. ___

MOON RIVER

from the Paramount Picture BREAKFAST AT TIFFANY'S

RECORDER

Words by JOHNNY MERCER
Music by HENRY MANCINI

MORNING HAS BROKEN

Recorder

Words by ELEANOR FARJEON
Music by CAT STEVENS

MY CHERIE AMOUR

Recorder

Words and Music by STEVIE WONDER,
SYLVIA MOY and HENRY COSBY

MY GIRL

RECORDER

Words and Music by WILLIAM "SMOKEY" ROBINSON
and RONALD WHITE

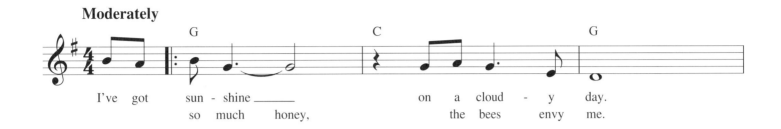

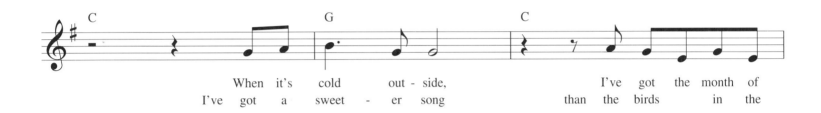

I've got sun - shine _____ on a cloud - y day.
so much honey, the bees envy me.

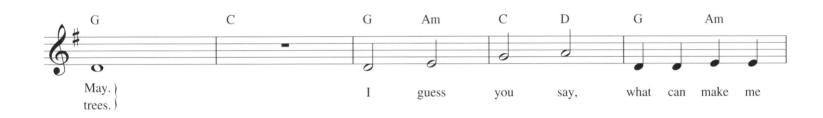

When it's cold out - side, I've got the month of
I've got a sweet - er song than the birds in the

May. ⎫
trees. ⎭ I guess you say, what can make me

feel this way? My girl. (My girl, my girl.) Talk - in' 'bout

Am7
1.
D7
2.
D7 G

my girl. _____ (My girl.) I've got (My girl.)

MY FAVORITE THINGS

from THE SOUND OF MUSIC

RECORDER

Lyrics by OSCAR HAMMERSTEIN II
Music by RICHARD RODGERS

Brightly

Rain - drops on ros - es and whis - kers on kit - tens,
Cream - col - ored po - nies and crisp ap - ple stru - dels,

bright cop - per ket - tles and warm wool - en mit - tens,
door - bells and sleigh - bells and schnit - zel with noo - dles,

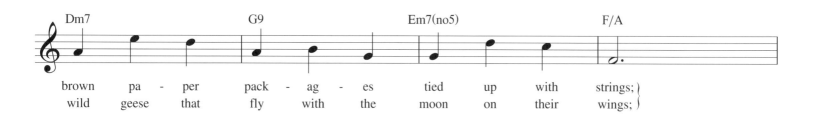

brown pa - per pack - ag - es tied up with strings;
wild geese that fly with the moon on their wings;

these are a few of my fa - vor - ite things.

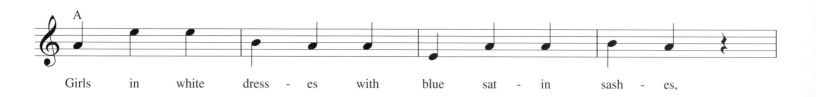

Girls in white dress - es with blue sat - in sash - es,

MY HEART WILL GO ON
(Love Theme from 'Titanic')
from the Paramount and Twentieth Century Fox Motion Picture TITANIC

RECORDER

Music by JAMES HORNER
Lyric by WILL JENNINGS

NIGHTS IN WHITE SATIN

RECORDER

Words and Music by
JUSTIN HAYWARD

NOWHERE MAN

RECORDER

Words and Music by JOHN LENNON
and PAUL McCARTNEY

PUFF THE MAGIC DRAGON

RECORDER

Words and Music by LENNY LIPTON
and PETER YARROW

RAINDROPS KEEP FALLIN' ON MY HEAD

from BUTCH CASSIDY AND THE SUNDANCE KID

RECORDER

Lyric by HAL DAVID
Music by BURT BACHARACH

SCARBOROUGH FAIR/CANTICLE

RECORDER

Arrangement and Original Counter Melody by PAUL SIMON
and ARTHUR GARFUNKEL

Moderately fast

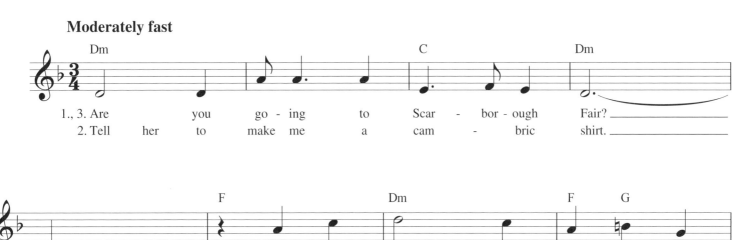

1., 3. Are you go - ing to Scar - bor - ough Fair? _____
2. Tell her to make me a cam - bric shirt. _____

_____ Pars - ley, sage, rose - mar - y and
_____ Pars - ley, sage, rose - mar - y and

thyme. _____ Re -
thyme. _____ With -

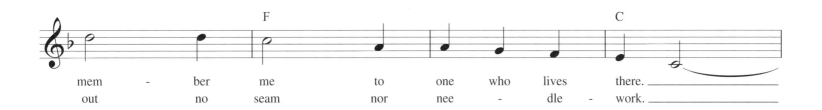

mem - ber me to one who lives there. _____
out no seam nor nee - dle - work. _____

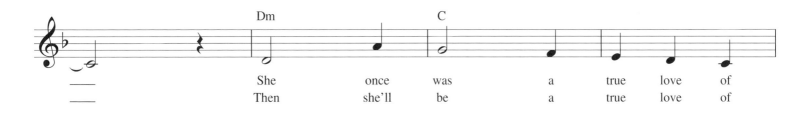

She once was a true love of
Then she'll be a true love of

mine. _____
mine. _____

Somewhere Out There

from AN AMERICAN TAIL

Recorder

Music by BARRY MANN and JAMES HORNER
Lyric by CYNTHIA WEIL

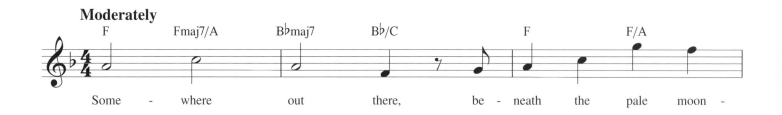

Some - where out there, be - neath the pale moon -

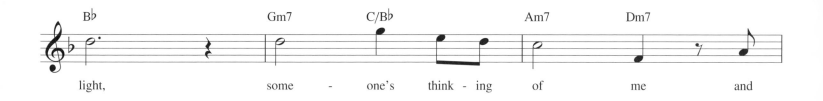

light, some - one's think - ing of me and

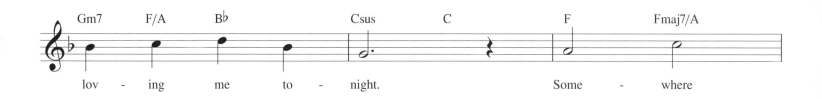

lov - ing me to - night. Some - where

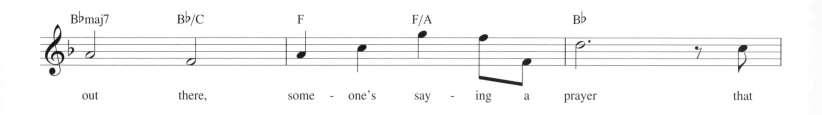

out there, some - one's say - ing a prayer that

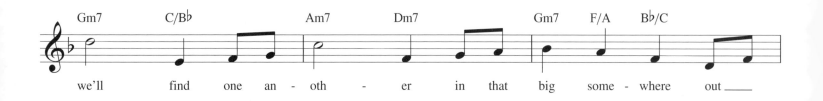

we'll find one an - oth - er in that big some - where out ____

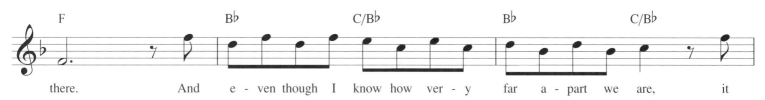

there. And e - ven though I know how ver - y far a - part we are, it

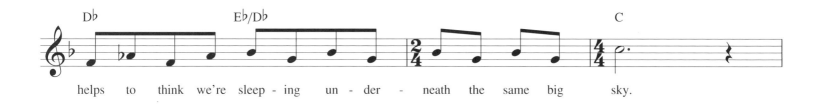

helps to think we might be wish - ing on the same bright star. And

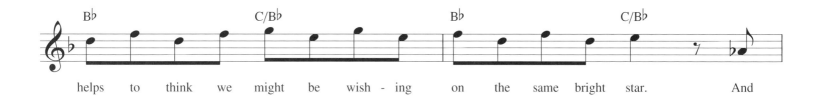

when the night wind starts to sing that lone - some lull - a - by, it

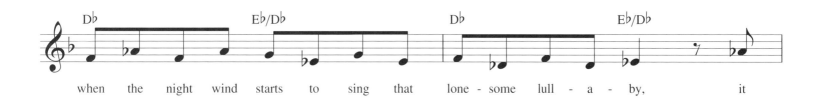

helps to think we're sleep - ing un - der - neath the same big sky.

Some - where out there, if love can see us

through, then we'll be to - geth - er some - where

out there, out where dreams come true.

THE SOUND OF MUSIC
from THE SOUND OF MUSIC

RECORDER

Lyrics by OSCAR HAMMERSTEIN II
Music by RICHARD RODGERS

Moderately

The hills are a - live with the sound of mu - sic, _____ with

songs they have sung for a thou - sand years. _____ The

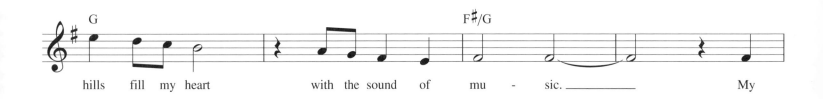

hills fill my heart with the sound of mu - sic. _____ My

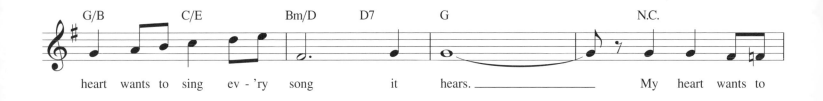

heart wants to sing ev - 'ry song it hears. _____ My heart wants to

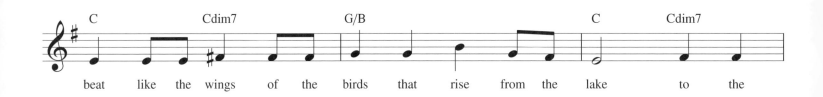

beat like the wings of the birds that rise from the lake to the

trees. My heart wants to sigh like a chime that flies from a

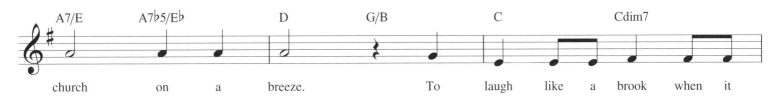

church   on   a   breeze.   To   laugh   like   a   brook   when   it

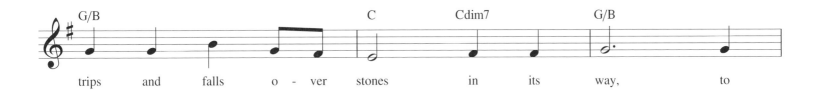

trips   and   falls   o - ver   stones   in   its   way,   to

sing   through   the   night   like   a   lark   who   is   learn - ing   to   pray.   I

go   to   the   hills   when   my   heart   is   lone - ly.   I

know   I   will   hear   what I've heard   be - fore.   My

heart   will   be   blessed   with   the   sound   of   mu - sic,   and   I'll

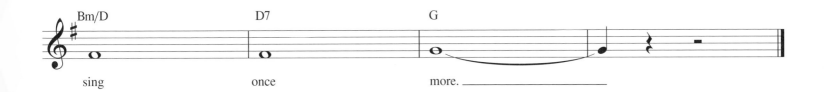

sing   once   more.

STRANGERS IN THE NIGHT
adapted from A MAN COULD GET KILLED

Recorder

Words by CHARLES SINGLETON and EDDIE SNYDER
Music by BERT KAEMPFERT

SUNSHINE ON MY SHOULDERS

RECORDER

Words by JOHN DENVER
Music by JOHN DENVER, MIKE TAYLOR
and DICK KNISS

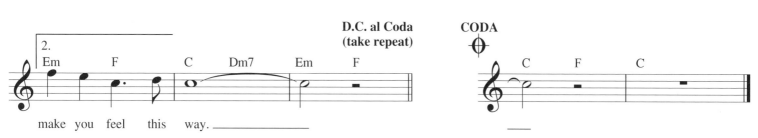

SWEET CAROLINE

RECORDER

Words and Music by
NEIL DIAMOND

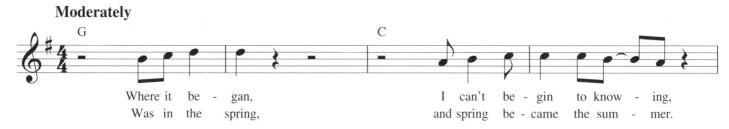

Where it be - gan,   I can't be - gin to know - ing,
Was in the spring,   and spring be - came the sum - mer.

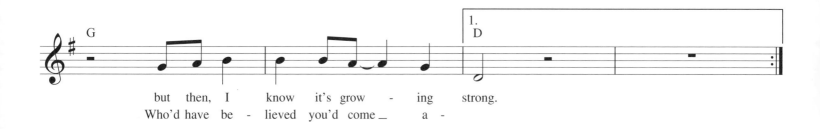

but then, I know it's grow - ing strong.
Who'd have be - lieved you'd come ___ a -

long.   Hands, _____   touch-ing hands, _____

reach-ing out,   touch-ing me,   touch-ing you. _____

Sweet Car - o - line, ___   good times nev - er seemed so
I've been in - clined ___   to be - lieve they nev - er

good.   would. Oh, no, no.

TILL THERE WAS YOU

from Meredith Willson's THE MUSIC MAN

RECORDER

By MEREDITH WILLSON

THE TIMES THEY ARE A-CHANGIN'

RECORDER

Words and Music by
BOB DYLAN

UNCHAINED MELODY

RECORDER

Lyric by HY ZARET
Music by ALEX NORTH

TOMORROW
from The Musical Production ANNIE

Recorder

Lyric by MARTIN CHARNIN
Music by CHARLES STROUSE

Moderately fast

The sun - 'll come out to - mor - row. Bet your bot - tom

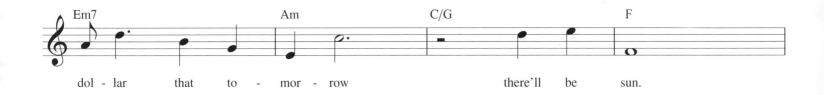

dol - lar that to - mor - row there'll be sun.

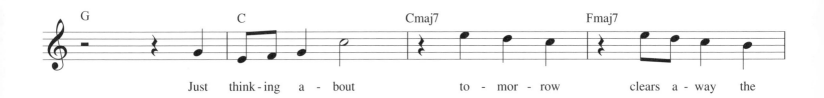

Just think - ing a - bout to - mor - row clears a - way the

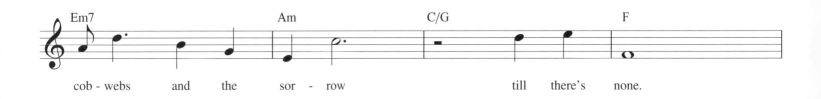

cob - webs and the sor - row till there's none.

When I'm stuck with a day that's gray and lone - ly,

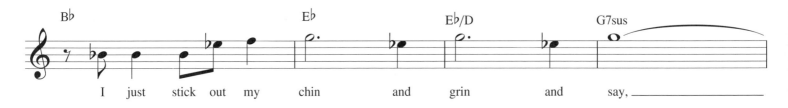

I just stick out my chin and grin and say, _____

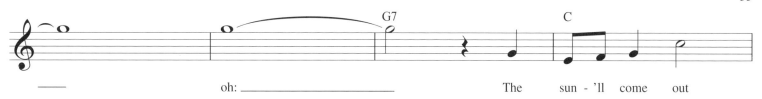

oh: _____ The sun -'ll come out

to - mor - row, so you got - ta hang on till to - mor - row,

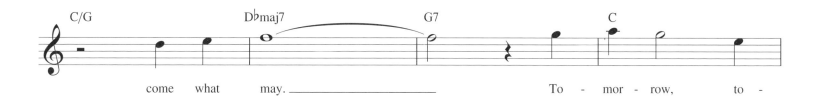

come what may. _____ To - mor - row, to -

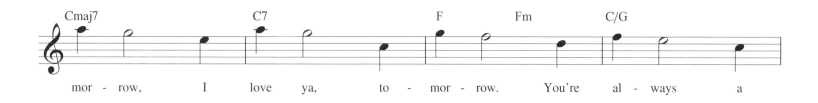

mor - row, I love ya, to - mor - row. You're al - ways a

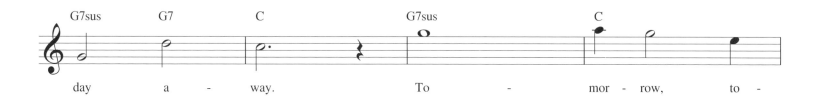

day a - way. To - mor - row, to -

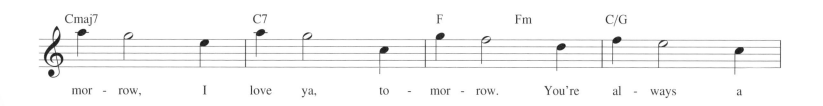

mor - row, I love ya, to - mor - row. You're al - ways a

day _____ a - way! _____

VIVA LA VIDA

Words and Music by GUY BERRYMAN,
JON BUCKLAND, WILL CHAMPION
and CHRIS MARTIN

Recorder

Moderately

I used to rule the world. ___ Seas would rise when I gave the word. ___

___ Now in the morn-ing I sleep a - lone, ___ sweep the

streets I used to own. ___

I used to roll the dice, ___ feel the

fear in my en - e - my's eyes, ___ lis - ten as the crowd ___ would sing, ___

___ "Now the old king is dead; ___ long live the king." One min - ute I

held the key, ___ next the walls were closed on

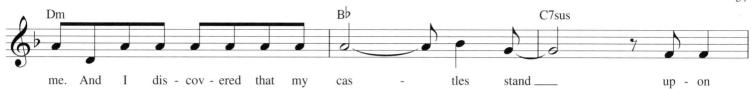

me. And I dis - cov - ered that my cas - tles stand ____ up - on

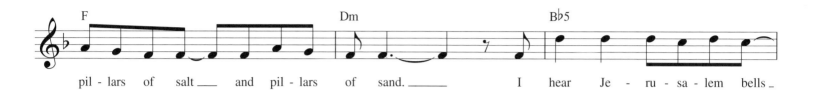

pil - lars of salt ____ and pil - lars of sand. _____ I hear Je - ru - sa - lem bells _

____ a - ring - ing. Ro - man cav - al - ry choirs ____ are sing - ing.

Be my mir - ror, my sword ____ and shield, _____ my mis - sion - ar - ies in a for -

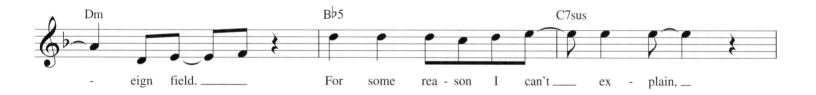

- eign field. _____ For some rea - son I can't ____ ex - plain, __

once you've gone there was nev - er, nev - er an hon - est word, __

____ and that was when I ruled the world. ___

WE ARE THE WORLD

RECORDER

Words and Music by LIONEL RICHIE
and MICHAEL JACKSON

WHAT A WONDERFUL WORLD

RECORDER

Words and Music by GEORGE DAVID WEISS
and BOB THIELE

WONDERWALL

RECORDER

Words and Music by
NOEL GALLAGHER

_____ the lights _ that lead _____ us there _ are blind - ing.

There are man - y things _____ that I _____ would like to say to you, _

_____ but I don't know how. _____

Be - cause may - be _____ you're gon -

- na be the one that saves me, _____ and

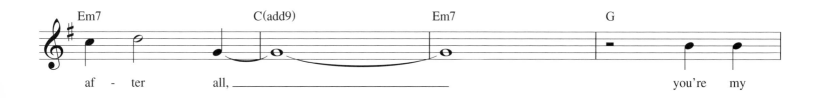

af - ter all, _____ you're my

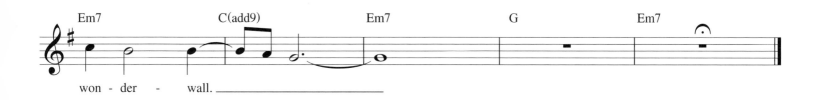

won - der - wall. _____

YOU ARE THE SUNSHINE OF MY LIFE

RECORDER

Words and Music by
STEVIE WONDER

You are the sun - shine of ___ my life. ___
You are the ap - ple of ___ my eye. ___

That's why I'll al - ways be ___ a - round. ___
For - ev - er you'll ___ stay in ___ my heart. ___

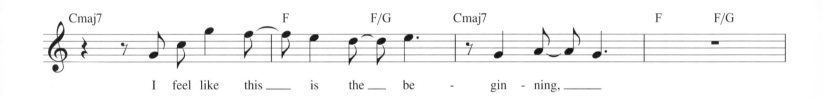

I feel like this ___ is the ___ be - gin - ning, ___

though I've loved you ___ for a thou - sand years. ___

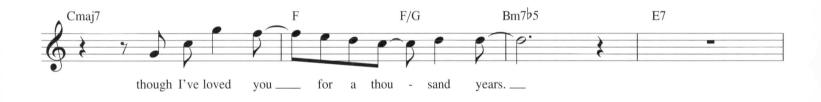

And if I thought ___ our love ___ was end - ing, ___ I'd find ___

___ my - self ___ drown - ing in my ___ own tears. Whoa, ___ whoa. ___

YOU'VE GOT A FRIEND

RECORDER

Words and Music by
CAROLE KING